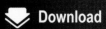
C000133621

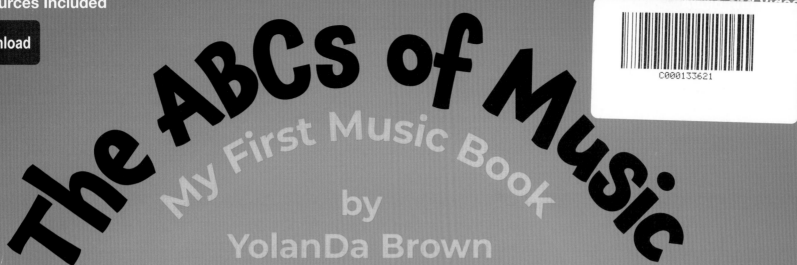

The ABCs of Music
My First Music Book
by
YolanDa Brown

PLAYBACK+
Speed • Pitch • Balance • Loop

To access audio, video, and PDF resources, visit:
www.halleonard.com/mylibrary

4884-5378-2493-4778

Illustrations of YolanDa by Sergio Sandoval.

ISBN: 978-1-70510-889-5

Visit Hal Leonard Online at
www.halleonard.com

Contact us:
Hal Leonard
7777 West Bluemound Road
Milwaukee, WI 53213
Email: info@halleonard.com

In Europe, contact:
Hal Leonard Europe Limited
42 Wigmore Street
Marylebone, London, W1U 2RY
Email: info@halleonardeurope.com

In Australia, contact:
Hal Leonard Australia Pty. Ltd.
4 Lentara Court
Cheltenham, Victoria, 3192 Australia
Email: info@halleonard.com.au

Preface

My mission is to make every child's first encounter of music intriguing and fun. Discovering music should be an engaging process; a lifelong journey full of possibility and wonder. This book is a first stepping stone in that journey.

Music has been a part of my life for as long as I can remember. My Dad played all kinds of music on his record player, from reggae to country and everything in between. You name it, he had it in his collection. I loved moving to these exciting sounds, but I just couldn't wait to start making music and finding a voice of my own!

I played the piano from the age of six and then later added the violin and drums. At the age of 13, I started learning the saxophone and I knew that it would become my favourite instrument. I feel very lucky that it is now my job to tour the world and play music to people everywhere.

I am often asked how to begin learning about music. *The ABCs of Music* aims to be the "go-to" for children, parents, and schools who are curious about encountering music for the first time. On our musical adventure together, we will listen, play games, and learn about a variety of musical genres and instruments. Through these activities, I want each child to discover their "Musical Me"; a unique musical identity made up of likes, dislikes, feelings, and skills. Just like my Dad's record collection did for me, I hope that this book introduces a rainbow of music into your lives!

YolanDa Brown

For Parents, Carers, and Teachers

1. Creating

Learning about music means making music. Encourage your child to engage with a musical instrument when looking at this book's various activities. It can be a piano, toy keyboard, piano app, or even a toy xylophone or glockenspiel. Don't forget, the voice is also a musical instrument. There are opportunities for music-making throughout this book, so go for it!

2. Sharing

Music is learnt best as a shared experience. There will be opportunities in this book for your child to listen to music and explore their own musical preferences and identities. Encourage them to talk with you about their feelings and opinions. Share your own!

3. Collaborating

At the heart of a musical experience is communicating and having fun together. So, join in with your child and get creative, giving lots of positive feedback and encouragement along the way.

4. Music is for Everyone

You don't have to be a music specialist to enjoy music or facilitate musical experiences for children. Just like you don't have to be an author to inspire a love for reading! There is plenty of guidance throughout the book and you can have fun learning, too! A shared journey of discovery with your child is very precious and powerful.

How to Use This Book

Throughout this book, there will be interactive musical games and activities to engage your child. Just look out for the ✏ symbol, which will prompt you to get active. Use a nice, sharp pencil and have an eraser to hand.

Your book also contains opportunities for listening to lots of great music and downloadable resources. To access the accompanying audio and additional PDF activities, simply look for the 🔊 ⬇ Download icons, go to **www.halleonard.com/mylibrary**, and enter the code found on page 1 of this book. YolanDa's welcome video is here, too (look for the ▶ icon on page 3).

For even more music, you can listen to *The ABCs of Music* Spotify playlists, hosted by Hal Leonard and curated by YolanDa herself. You can access the playlists using the codes on pages 38–39.

This Book Belongs To

_____

My Drawing of Me

Chapter 1:
Welcome to Music!

> Hello and welcome to music! I'm Yolanda, and together we are going to learn about music and how it's made!

We are about to go on a wonderful journey together, learning about musical instruments, types of music, the musical alphabet, and different elements of music (such as rhythm and melody). There will be lots of activities for you to have a go at. Just look out for the  symbol! You'll also have a chance to discover your "Musical Me," made up of your likes, dislikes, feelings, and skills.

And don't forget to check out the Did You Know? sections, with loads of awesome facts about music!

Remember that music is all about having fun, so don't worry if things seem tricky at first. We'll learn together, step by step. The amazing thing about this book is that, once you've had a go at all the activities, it will be completely unique to you. There won't be another book like it in the whole world!

Musical Me

Let's explore what you like about music!

I Like Music Because

_____

_____

_____

My Favourite Piece of Music Is

_____

_____

_____

My Musical Doodles

Now, listen to your favourite piece of music. While you listen, draw some doodles or words in the space opposite. When the music is over, talk about your doodles with a grown-up.

Why not ask a grown-up to doodle to their favourite piece of music? Ask them to explain their pictures with you!

Chapter 2:
Musical Instruments

All the sound we need to make music comes from musical instruments. Musical instruments create sound by making the air around them **vibrate** (meaning the air shakes really fast, creating sound that our ears can hear).

With musical instruments, the bigger

or longer

the instrument, the lower it plays.

The smaller the instrument, the higher it plays!

Musical instruments are grouped together into families or sections. Each instrumental family has its own name and all the instruments in that family share characteristics (e.g., the material they are made of and how they are played).

Read about the instrumental families over the page and listen to what the instruments sound like!

Did you know?

One of the oldest musical instruments we know about is a flute made from mammoth ivory. It's over 40,000 years old!

Percussion

- A percussion instrument is anything that should be hit, scraped, or shaken to make a sound. Hands or special beaters help to create the sound.

- Some percussion instruments help groups of musicians to stay together and play in time. Others are able to play specific **pitches** (high and low musical notes) and can even play tunes.

Pitched Percussion (these instruments can play high and low notes)

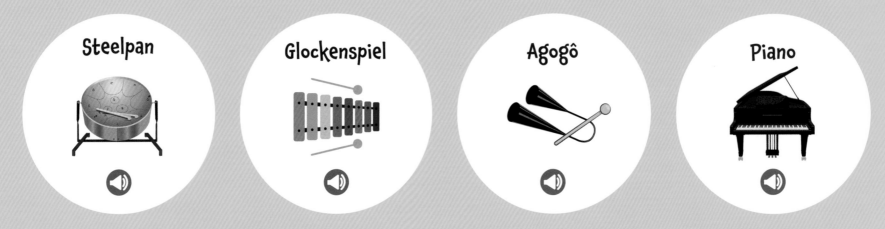

Steelpan   Glockenspiel   Agogô   Piano

Unpitched Percussion (these instruments create sound but not pitches)

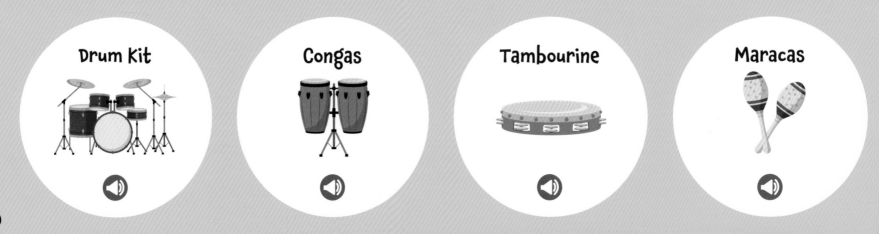

Drum Kit   Congas   Tambourine   Maracas

Wind

- Wind instruments make a sound when air is blown through them. A musician can play different notes by covering holes on the instrument with their fingers or by pressing keys that cover the holes.

- Some wind instruments use a reed to make a sound. The musician's breath makes the reed vibrate. Other wind instruments don't have a reed. The player blows across or into a hole.

Wind Instruments With a Reed

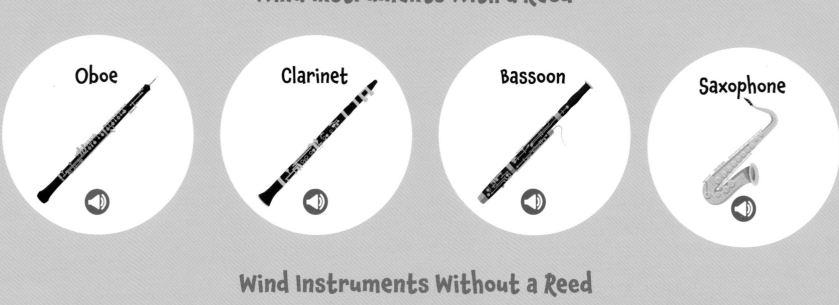

Oboe

Clarinet

Bassoon

Saxophone

Wind Instruments Without a Reed

Flute

Recorder

Ocarina

Did You Know?

The saxophone is made of brass but is in the wind family because it uses a reed to produce sound.

Brass

- A brass instrument is—you've guessed it—made of brass! You create notes by blowing down a mouthpiece, changing the position of your lips, and pressing down buttons called valves.

Trumpet

Trombone

French Horn

Electric Instruments

- These instruments rely on electricity to produce sound. The electricity can control how loud or soft the instrument is, as well as adding interesting effects to create cool, new sounds.

Did You know?

Computers also produce music. They are used in recording studios to record sounds and musicians can even create music on them!

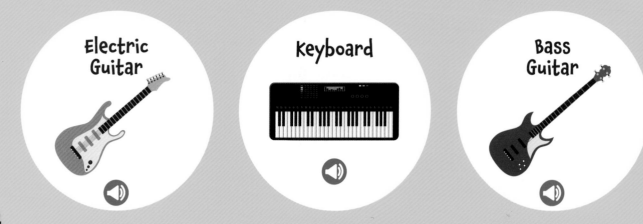

Electric Guitar

Keyboard

Bass Guitar

Strings

- You make a sound on these instruments either by plucking a string with your finger or moving a bow along the string to make it vibrate. (A bow is a wooden stick with horsehair attached.) These instruments are usually hollow and made of wood.

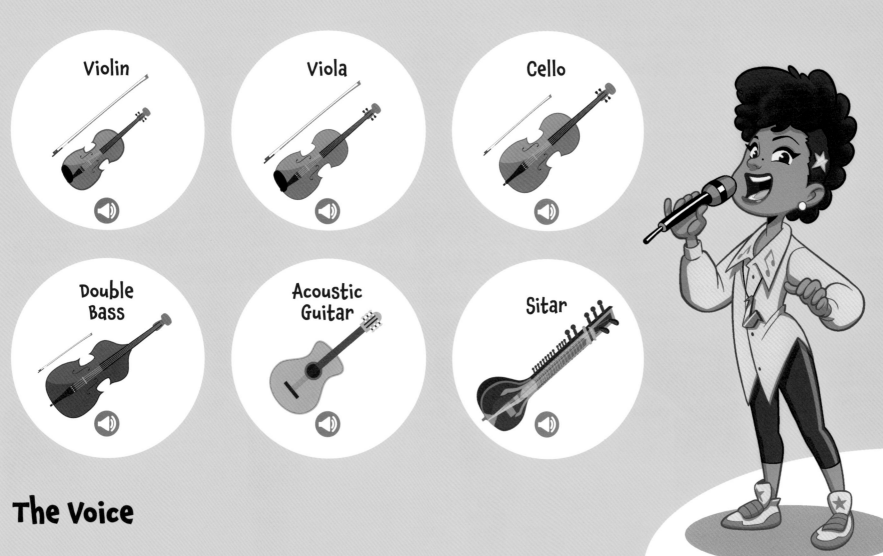

Violin

Viola

Cello

Double Bass

Acoustic Guitar

Sitar

The Voice

- The voice is an amazing instrument because we all have it! Singing is so fun to do. You can sing on your own, in a **band**, or with a group of other singers called a **choir**.

Voice

Musical Me

My Favourite Percussion Instrument: _____

My Favourite Wind Instrument: _____

My Favourite Brass Instrument: _____

My Favourite Electric Instrument: _____

My Favourite String Instrument: _____

The Family Home

Here are the houses for three instrumental families. In the spaces provided, write in two instruments that belong in each family home from the choices below.

Steelpan
Bass Guitar
Trombone
Keyboard
Congas
Trumpet

Brass   Electric   Percussion

Chapter 3:
Types of Music

There are so many different types of music from all around the world. Some types of music can be loud and fast, and make you want to get up and dance. Others can be slow and quiet, and make you want to relax. The most important thing is to listen to as many different types of music as possible. So, let's go!

Classical and Opera

YolanDa's Facts

- Western classical music originated in Europe over 600 years ago. There are lots of amazing classical composers writing music today.

- Classical music is usually performed by an **orchestra** or groups of different instruments and singers.

- An orchestra can have as many as 100 musicians playing at once but doesn't have any singers.

- Opera is performed by singers in a theatre with an orchestra. The singers also have to act and the storylines can be very dramatic!

Listen Here! YolanDa's Classical Audio

Jazz and Blues

YolanDa's Facts

- Blues music originated in West Africa and became established in the late 19th century in the United States of America. Jazz and Blues is often **improvised**, which means musicians make up what they are going to play on the spot. Wow!

- Jazz can be played by a **big band** of over 20 musicians as well as by small groups like a **trio** (three musicians).

Listen Here! YolanDa's Jazz and Blues Audio

Rock

YolanDa's Facts

- Rock music began in the Unites States of America in the mid-1950s.

- This music is played by a combination of electric guitars, drums, keyboard, and voices. It is loud and full of energy. The guitar is the most important sound that you hear in rock music. When listening to rock music, a lot of people pretend to play the guitar without an instrument (called playing "air guitar"). Give it a try!

Listen Here! YolanDa's Rock Audio

Pop

YolanDa's Facts

- Pop music began in the 1950s, when types of rock 'n' roll music started reaching more people.

- Pop stands for "popular" and millions of people all over the world listen to this type of music.

Listen Here! YolanDa's Pop Audio

Reggae

YolanDa's Facts

- Reggae music came from Jamaica in the late 1960s. It then became music that much of the world loved!

- The bass line and the drumbeat are very important in Reggae, giving the music its unique sound.

Listen Here! YolanDa's Reggae Audio

Country

YolanDa's Facts

- Country music originated in the 1920s in the south of the United States of America.

- The guitar is one of the most important instruments in country music, and songs often tell stories about life, family, and love.

Listen Here! YolanDa's Country Audio

Did You know?

Types of music are called **genres**. You can even mix different genres together to make new styles and sounds. For example, latin and jazz make the genre "latin jazz."

Hip Hop/Rap

YolanDa's Facts

- Hip Hop came from New York City in the United States of America and dates back to the 1970s.

- It has catchy, strong rhythms and musicians often take parts of other songs to use in their own music (called **sampling**).

- Rapping means to speak words in a rhythmic manner, rather than singing. Often, people rap in rhymes or rap very quickly over a drumbeat. You will often hear rapping in between passages of singing.

Listen Here! YolanDa's Hip Hop/Rap Audio

Here are some more types of music you can discover!

- **Afrobeats**
- **Bollywood**
- **Folk**
- **Gospel**
- **K-Pop**
- **Latin**
- **Musical Theatre**
- **Rock 'n' Roll**
- **Soul/R&B**

If you want to listen to more examples of musical genres, check out YolanDa's *The ABCs of Music* playlists on Spotify. You can access them on pages 38-39.

Musical Me

Listen through to the types of music again and complete the activities. Once you've shared your responses, why not ask friends and family to take part? It's so interesting to listen and talk about music together!

The Type of Music That Makes Me Want to Dance Is

_____

The Type of Music That Makes Me Relaxed Is

_____

My Top Three Musical Genres Are:

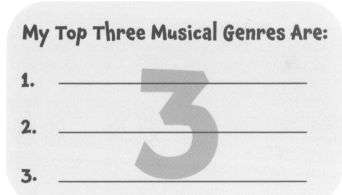

1. _____

2. _____

3. _____

My Doodles and Words

Listen back to a genre of music. Draw doodles and write some words that express how the music makes you feel.

Chapter 4: The Musical Alphabet

Did You Know?

It is thought that the earliest examples of written music come from Asia and are around 4,000 years old!

Music is a language with its own alphabet.

The **musical alphabet** contains seven main notes: C, D, E, F, G, A, and B. Each letter represents a note. Here is the musical alphabet on a piano keyboard.

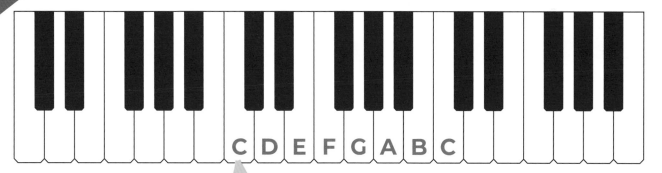

C D E F G A B C

This pattern of notes repeats again and again as you go further up the piano keyboard.

You can find the note C on a keyboard by looking for the grouping of two black keys next to each other. The note C is always immediately to the left of the first black key in this group.

If you can, find and play these notes on a piano, keyboard, piano app, or pitched percussion. Ask a grown-up to help. You can also listen to all the notes of the musical alphabet one after another here!

The Musical Alphabet

But how do musicians know which notes to play?

Many musicians understand what to play by listening to others, then copying and adapting what they hear. Often, musicians in an orchestra, choir, or band have all the music they need to play printed on paper. This is called **sheet music**.

A musical note looks like a dot. To make it easier to see which notes are higher or lower than others, musical notes are written on a set of five lines and four spaces called a **stave** or **staff**. At the beginning of this is a **clef sign** to name the lines and spaces. The clef sign we'll use together is called the **treble clef**.

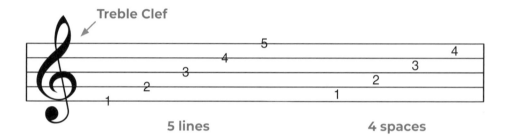

Treble Clef

5 lines   4 spaces

Each line and space on the stave has a letter name of its own. It's easy to remember the names of the lines and spaces. From bottom to the top, the lines are: E-G-B-D-F. One way to remember this is to say, "Every Green Bus Drives Fast."

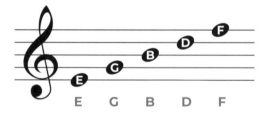

E   G   B   D   F

From bottom to top, the spaces are: F-A-C-E. This is easy to remember because the names of the spaces spell "face."

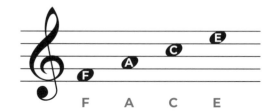

F   A   C   E

Imagine that the stave is like a ladder. A dot that is on a high line or space is a high note. A dot that is on a low line or space is a low note!

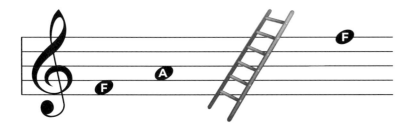

If a note is too high or too low to fit on the stave, extra lines can be added. These short lines are called **ledger lines**.

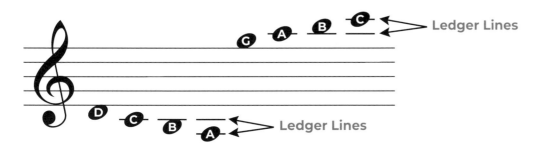

Ledger Lines

Ledger Lines

Did You know?

Sheet music for drum kits works slightly differently. Each line on the stave represents a different drum and there are different symbols for the cymbals!

Did You know?

To make reading the notes easier for you, we've added letters inside the noteheads. When you come to write your own music in this book, you won't have to do this!

Musical Me

You can tell how high or low a note is by its position on the stave. Circle the highest and lowest note in each of these examples. The first one has been done for you, with the lowest note circled yellow and the highest note circled red.

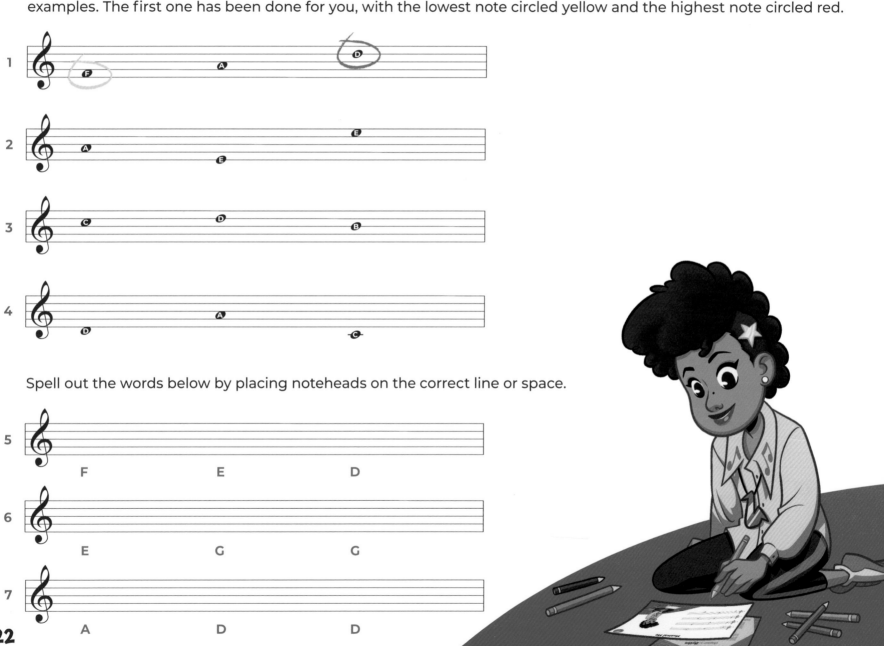

1 — F, A, D

2 — A, E, E

3 — C, D, B

4 — D, A, C

Spell out the words below by placing noteheads on the correct line or space.

5 — F, E, D

6 — E, G, G

7 — A, D, D

Chapter 5: Rhythm

Musical notes can be long or short. We use the word **rhythm** to describe the patterns of long and short notes in a piece of music. Rhythm can make you want to get up and dance. It can also make you want to relax.

It's easy to hear rhythm when we listen to drums play on a song. Listen to these rhythms played on a drum kit.

Drum Rhythms

Note Values

A musical note on a stave shows two things; how high or low a sound is and how long the sound lasts. Each type of note has a specific rhythmic value. Note values are measured in **beats**. When you tap your foot or clap your hands along with a song, you are tapping or clapping the **beat**. The most common note value is called a crotchet (or quarter note). When the beat is a crotchet/quarter note, all the other rhythmic values are determined by it.

Crotchet/Quarter Note

Lasts for
one beat.

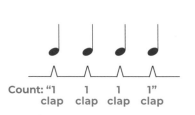

Minim/Half Note

Fills the time of two
crotchets/quarter notes.

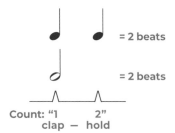

Semibreve/Whole Note

Fills the time of four
crotchets/quarter notes.

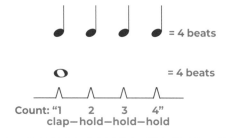

23

Remember, the stave (or staff) shows us how high or low musical notes are.

Here is a stave with some added symbols. These make it easier for us to read the notes. The **double bar** tells us when the music has finished.

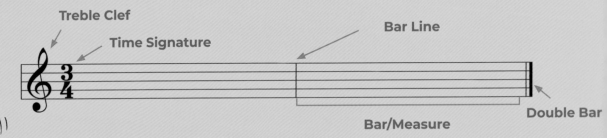

Treble Clef
Time Signature
Bar Line
Bar/Measure
Double Bar

Bar lines divide music into units called **bars** or **measures**. The **time signature** tells us the number of beats per bar.

Counting

4 beats per bar

1 2 3 4 1 2 3 4 1 2 3 4

The music above has a $\frac{4}{4}$ time signature. We call this "four-four." The number "4" on top means there are four beats in each bar. The bottom "4" tells us that the beat has the value of a crotchet/quarter note.

Now, listen to this piece of music. Count along, saying, "1-2-3-4." You'll hear me say, "1-2-3-4" before the music begins. This is the beat.

Counting in $\frac{4}{4}$ Audio

Rests

Rests are musical symbols that stand for silence. A rest will indicate when *not* to play a note. Like notes, each rest is worth a certain number of beats, as shown below.

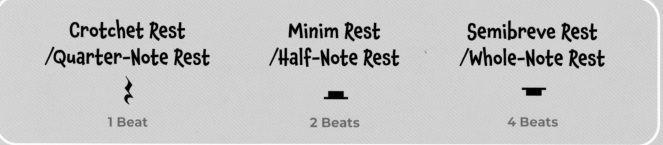

Crotchet Rest /Quarter-Note Rest	Minim Rest /Half-Note Rest	Semibreve Rest /Whole-Note Rest
1 Beat	2 Beats	4 Beats

Quavers/Eighth Notes

The last note value we are going to discover is the quaver or eighth note.

A single quaver/eighth note has a flag. When two or more appear together, the flags turn into beams. When the time signature is $\frac{4}{4}$, they are often connected in groups of two or four. The beams make reading music easier.

Two quavers/eighth notes fill the time of one crotchet/quarter-note beat.

When we count quavers/eighth notes, it's easier if we tap our feet together. Here is my foot, tapping along to a beat.

Count "1-2-3-4" and tap along with me! As we tap, we move our feet up and down, tapping on the floor for each beat. To count quavers/eighth notes, we tap the same way but the notes sound twice as fast.

Count: 1 & 2 & 3 & 4 &

The "ands" are when I raise my foot.

Try it yourself, tapping your foot and counting "1 & 2 & 3 & 4 &."

Clap and count the rhythm below, which contains a quaver/eighth-note rest. Here is the rest symbol for a quaver/eighth note: ♪ . It has the same value as the note.

You can listen to the rhythm here!   Counting "ands" Audio

Musical Me

Add the Missing Bar Lines

Bar lines divide music into units called bars or measures. The time signature tells us how many beats are in each bar.

First, note the time signature in each example. How many beats should be in each bar?
Then, use bar lines to group the music into bars.

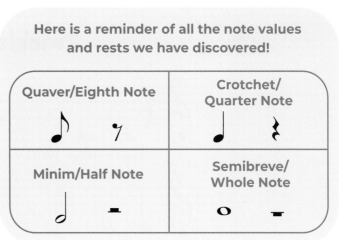

Here is a reminder of all the note values and rests we have discovered!

Quaver/Eighth Note	Crotchet/Quarter Note
♪ 𝄾	♩ 𝄽
Minim/Half Note	**Semibreve/Whole Note**
𝅗𝅥 ▬	𝅝 ▬

True or False?

Circle **T** for true or **F** for false after considering the following musical sums!

1. T F ♪♪ = ♩

2. T F ♪♪ + ♩ = 𝅗𝅥

3. T F 𝄾 + ♪ + ♩ = 𝅝

4. T F 𝄾 + 𝄾 = ♩

5. T F ♪ + ♪ + 𝄾 = 𝅝

Chapter 6: Melody

A **melody** is the part of a piece of music you sing or hum along to. A melody can also be known as a "tune." The best melodies are often easy to remember.

Here are some popular melodies. You can listen to the melodies using the online audio and sing along with me. Why not even try following the sheet music? Let's make music together!

Did You know?

The oldest known **melody** is the "Hurrian Hymn No.6." It is over 3,400 years old and was discovered carved into a clay tablet in Syria, Western Asia.

Happy Birthday

London Bridge Is Falling Down

Musical Me

Try to name the well-known melodies below. Some notes are missing, can you write them in? If you get stuck, have a listen to the complete melody online to help.

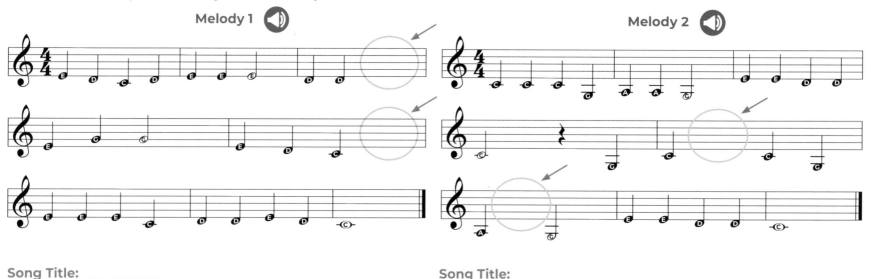

Melody 1

Melody 2

Song Title: _____

Song Title: _____

4 beats per bar

The beat is a crotchet/ quarter note

Make Your Own Melody!

Use the notes and rhythms we have learnt so far to write your own melody. The first and last notes have been written for you.

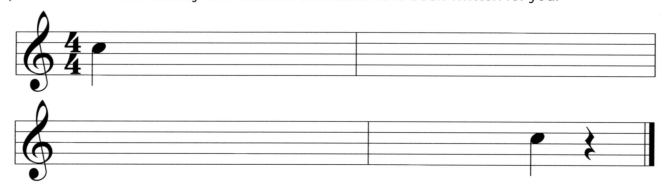

Then, go online and play your melody along with my band! (I'll count you in, saying, "1-2-3-4." This is the speed of the beat.)

Play Your Melody with YolanDa's Band!

Chapter 7: Fun and Games!

YolanDa's new drum kit has arrived! There are six differences between her new and old kits; can you find them all?

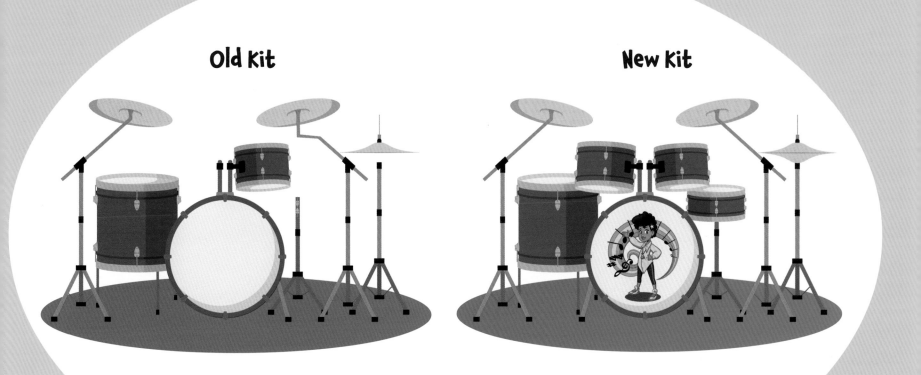

Old Kit

New Kit

Build YolanDa's Band!

YolanDa is singing in a concert and wants you to pick her band! Choose one instrument from each instrumental family to draw and colour in under the spotlights.

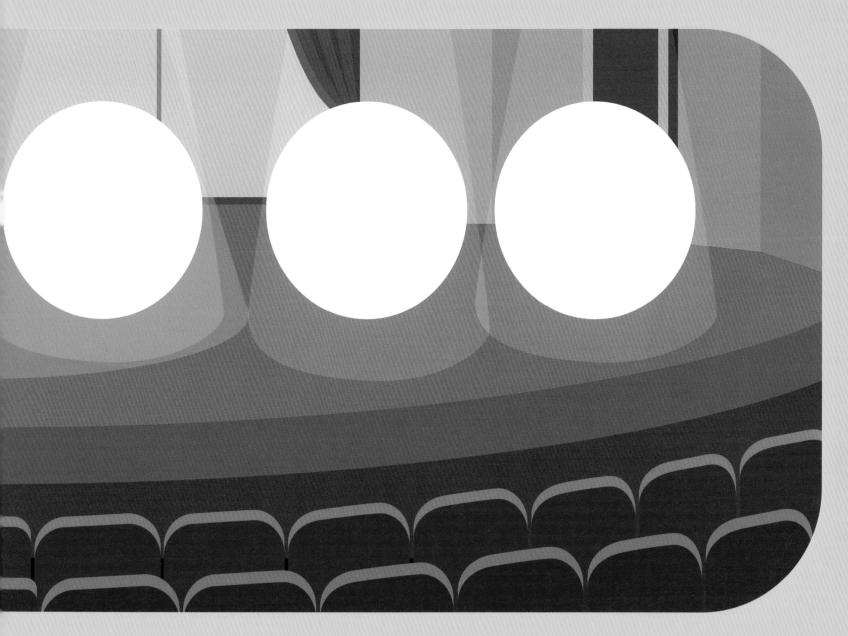

YolanDa's Musical Crossword

Can you help YolanDa complete her musical crossword? She's filled in some of the letters to help you!

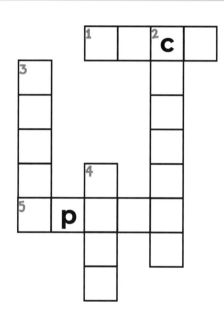

Across

1. The notes that fall in the four spaces of the treble clef spell _____ .

5. A type of music that involves singing, acting, and dramatic storylines.

Down

2. These are the letters of the musical alphabet.

3. A percussion instrument with keys, hammers, and strings.

4. A musical symbol that represents silence.

Do-It-Yourself Glossary

Complete the Glossary below by filling in the missing letters!

Term	Definition
B___nd	A medium-sized group of pop or rock instruments.
Be___t	The pulse in music that you clap or tap.
Cho___r	A group of singers.
Crotch___t/Quarter Note	A note value worth one beat.
G___nre	This means "type of music."
I___provise	To make up music on the spot.
Ledg___r Lines	Extra lines added under or above the stave/staff.
Melod___	The part of music that you sing or hum along to. Also known as a "tune."
Min___m/Half Note	A note value worth two beats.
Musical Al___ ___abet	The group of seven letter-names for musical notes.
Musi___ ___l Instrume___t	An object that produces musical sound.
Orch___str___	A big group of classical music instruments.
Pitc___	The high or low quality to a musical note.
Q___aver/Eighth Note	A note value worth half a crotchet/quarter note.
R___ ___thm	This word describes patterns of long and short notes in music.
Semibre___e/Whole Note	A note value worth four beats.
Sh___ ___t Music	Music that is printed on paper.
Stave/St___ ___f	The five lines and four spaces that musical notes are written on.
Time Sig___ ___tu___e	Numbers at the beginning of music that show the beats per bar.
Tre___le C___ef	The symbol at the start of music that names the lines and spaces on the stave/staff.
R___s___s	Symbols to show silence in music.

Answers

Page 14 **The Family Home**

Page 22 **Highest and Lowest Note**

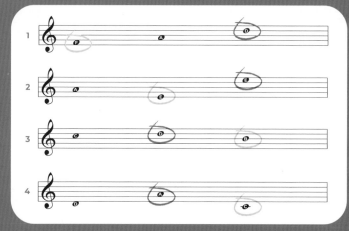

Page 22 **Notes on the Stave**

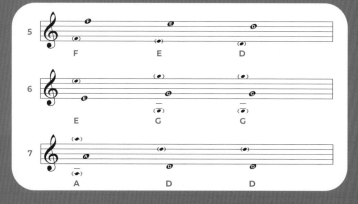

Page 27 **Add the Missing Bar Lines**

Page 27 **True or False?**

1. T   **2.** T   **3.** F   **4.** T   **5.** F

Page 30 **Melody Challenge**

Mary Had a Little Lamb

Page 30 **Melody Challenge Continued**

Old MacDonald Had a Farm

Page 31 **Spot the Difference**

Old Kit   New Kit

Page 34 **Yolanda's Musical Crossword**

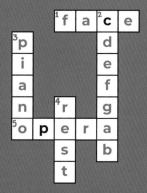

Page 35 **Do-It-Yourself Glossary**

Band, Beat, Choir, Crotchet/Quarter Note, Genre, Improvise, Ledger Lines, Melody, Minim/Half Note, Musical Alphabet, Musical Instrument, Orchestra, Pitch, Quaver/Eighth Note, Rhythm, Semibreve/Whole Note, Sheet Music, Stave/Staff, Time Signature, Treble Clef, Rests.

YolanDa's Playlists

It's so important to have an open mind and listen to as many different types of music as you can. Check out more examples of musical genres by listening to YolanDa's *The ABCs of Music* playlists on Spotify.

To access each playlist, simply open Spotify, select "search," and scan your chosen code via the camera icon.

Happy Listening!

Afrobeats

Country

Bollywood

Folk

Classical and Opera

Gospel

Hip Hop/Rap

Open 🟢 | Search 🔍 | Scan 📷

Pop

Open 🟢 | Search 🔍 | Scan 📷

Jazz and Blues

Open 🟢 | Search 🔍 | Scan 📷

Reggae

Open 🟢 | Search 🔍 | Scan 📷

K-Pop

Open 🟢 | Search 🔍 | Scan 📷

Rock

Open 🟢 | Search 🔍 | Scan 📷

Latin

Open 🟢 | Search 🔍 | Scan 📷

Rock 'n' Roll

Open 🟢 | Search 🔍 | Scan 📷

Musical Theatre

Open 🟢 | Search 🔍 | Scan 📷

Soul/R&B

Open 🟢 | Search 🔍 | Scan 📷

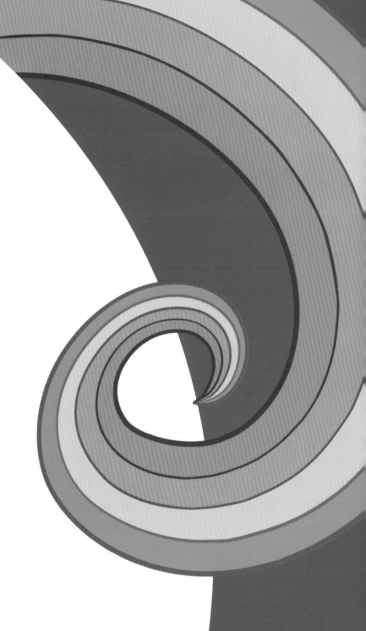

This is to certify that

_____

has completed **The ABCs of Music**
with flying colours!